SURFACE TO AIR SYSTEM
2019 WINTER MANUAL

A Compilation of Football Articles
Submitted by Rich Hargitt and S2A Members

The Surface to Air System

Books + Media

DEDICATION

From Rich Hargitt and Rick Butler —
co-founders of S2A

This compilation is dedicated to the tireless efforts of the football coaches that make up the membership of The Surface to Air System. We view our role in S2A as a service to a brotherhood that is a part of a larger group that make up the greatest profession in the world.

We are forever grateful to the men that volunteered their time, to put in print, and share their intellectual properties that make up the collective football thoughts that go into this work.

CONTENTS

Brian Brady - Head Coach Carson Graham Secondary - North Vancouver, Canada

Jacob Morris - Head Coach Grant County HS - Dry Ridge, KY

Sam Baker - Head Coach Grayslake North HS - Grayslake, IL

Rich Hargitt - Head Football Coach Emmett HS Emmett, ID

FOREWORD

I first met Rich Hargitt in the summer of 2018. We spoke over the phone a few times earlier in the spring about the Surface to Air System. That summer he was moving from South Carolina to Idaho to take a new football coaching position. One of his scheduled overnight stops on the journey was in Lincoln, NE. Less than 1 hour from my home and the school I had been the head coach at for 3 seasons. Rich and I scheduled to meet up in Lincoln early in the morning to talk football before his family was ready to hit the road. He told me his wife asked him where he met someone as crazy as he is to want to drive for an hour at 6:00 am to sit and talk football for 1 hour to then drive an hour back home.

We sat at a McDonald's diagramming schemes and adjustments on napkins. I had been using a run-heavy offense and needed something to mesh with my schemes to keep the defense honest. Coach Hargitt sold me on how S2A at its core is a spread RPO offensive system but it can be modified and adjusted to mesh with a variety of schemes. Coaches don't need to scrap everything they are currently doing because S2A is not an "all or none" thing.

He went through how he could foresee expanding my current package to be able to add packages from S2A. Over the course of the next two seasons and with tons of input from S2A members we are becoming more and more of an RPO team.

The S2A Manual is written by members sharing how they use the S2A system within their program. It is representative of the entire culture of S2A: sharing and caring. Coach Hargitt and Rick Butler set the standard for providing a true service to S2A members. They offer in-season weekly live webinars that give coaches a forum to share what they have done and what is working for their teams. Coaches are able to share their ideas and advice with each other. The whole group is one big family of coaches working together to improve each other's games as well as our own.

I hope this manual gives you some great football knowledge that you might use to tweak your schemes, maybe add a package or two, or even inspire you to go to something entirely new, like I did.

Brant Anderson
Head Football Coach
Thomas Jefferson HS
Council Bluffs, IA

INTRODUCTION

The 2019 edition of the Surface To Air System (S2A) Manual is a labor of love for our members and one that is close to each of our hearts. The members of S2A are not merely a consulting group or a group of like minded coaches or even a group of committed professionals, even though it is by definition all of those. The S2A is what we call "The Fraternity." This group cares deeply for the game of football and desires to make the game safer and more efficient for our student athletes. We discuss far ranging topics such as head injuries, team management, practice planning, schemes, and program development. The conversations and interactions that we have at our national clinic, on our webinars, and on or messaging app all allow our coaches to dialogue and network at a higher and more consistent level than had previously been possible.

This book is the next natural manifestation of that intense level of collaboration. When I wrote the first S2A Manual it was chiefly a product of my own thoughts and schemes and was principally just another discussion of my thoughts with the members within S2A.

It then became evident that the time had come to collaborate with our members and produce a book that was not so much my thoughts but instead a compilation of my thoughts with those of other coaches. As you peruse the pages of this book you will see that many of the chapters are written by S2A members as they outline their own unique twists on the system and how they have utilized and installed schemes in their own programs. This book is a proud and nostalgic step forward for S2A, and for me personally, as it is allowing great coaches that are loyal S2A members to publish their thoughts on offensive football in their own words for the world to see for the first time. I am honored and humbled to be able to support and to expose the thoughts of these great coaches and to get their words and messages out to the coaching community.

If you read these chapters and you are inspired to become a member of S2A to grow your knowledge and become a part of a group that cares for its members, please do not hesitate to reach out to us. We are very proud of our members and extremely excited to bring their thoughts and their successes to the forefront in this humble work. We hope you enjoy this book and that it contributes to your overall understanding of the game of football.

1.

Rick Butler - Co-Founder of the Surface to Air System

An open letter to Football Coaches: Stay in the Game

Dear Coach,

The chances are more than likely that a high percentage of you reading this open letter *have* either given serious thought, or *will* give serious thought to walking away from this profession within the next five years. Please take a deep breath if that is you at present, or consider sharing this with a coaching buddy that might be struggling with the same idea. As you continue to read these words, I ask that you do one thing, Remember. Remember what? Hang on, we are getting to that...

The common theme of this letter to you will be: Remember. This is the thought to hold onto in hopes that you will *Stay in the Game*.

If I could poll every coach that has hung up his whistle for the last time in the past ten years I would ask them to determine the common denominator for their eventual resignation. Although I cannot produce the results of that imaginary poll, I strongly believe we would all agree upon one common theme for getting out — burnout. Sure, there are a myriad of reasons given for walking away, such as:

- Finances
- Family
- Administration
- Undisciplined students
- Parents

The reasons listed are all just symptoms. Symptoms in medicine will tell a doctor what the sickness is. In coaching, the issues (symptoms) can lead to burnout (sickness). I dare say that anyone that has been in this profession, from a twenty year veteran to a freshly minted college graduate, has never been surprised by any one or a combination of these issues. Let's face it, to not have known things like "the money's not good, administrators can be fickle, or dealing with parents can be difficult" is either, quite frankly, naive or stupid.

Let's get back to *Remember*. I ask you to go back and remember why you got into coaching in the first place. Some call this your "why." I'll bet that most of the coaches that read this letter would include the word passion, or at least some phrase that would sum up your initial love (your "why") for getting in the game to coach. That initial zeal, I'm sure, left no doubt that this profession would be your calling.

The term "calling" reminds me of the greatest coaching movie ever produced, Rounders. Just kidding about it being a coaching flick, but still, Rounders' pivotal theme that made the production so meaningful to me, can and does apply to coaching. My favorite part of the movie is in the following dialog. Allow me to set the scene:

The movie Rounders was made in 1998. It starred Matt Damon as Mike, a young poker prodigy that is struggling between what the world is pressuring him to do — become a lawyer, and what he is passionate about — to sit at the table in Vegas and compete in the World Series of Poker.

The scene I am describing is between Mike and his law professor, Petrovsky. Mike enters a bar to apologize to his professor for missing an important law meeting from earlier in the day. The timeline of the scene portrays Mike in an internal struggle to fully commit and immerse himself as a law student, or to pursue what he cannot get out of his heart and mind - Poker.

Mike enters the bar and scans the room looking for Petrovsky. Upon reaching the professor's table, he is enthusiastically asked to sit down and join the old gentleman for a drink.

Professor:	Michael, may I tell you a story?
Mike:	Please.
Professor:	For generations men in my family have been Rabbis, in Israel, and before that, in Europe. It was to be my calling. I was quite a prodigy, the pride of my Yeshiva. The elders said I had a 40-year-olds understanding of

	the Midrash by the time I was 12. But by the time I was 13, I knew I could never be a rabbi.
Mike:	Why not?
Professor:	Because for all I understood of the Talmud, I never saw God there.
Mike:	You couldn't lie to yourself.
Professor:	I tried. Oh, I tried like crazy. I mean people were counting on me.
Mike:	Well, but yours is a respectable profession.
Professor:	Not to my family. My parents were destroyed, devastated by my decision. My father sent me away to New York to live with distant cousins. Eventually I found my place, my life's work.
Mike:	What then?
Professor:	Well I immersed myself fully. I studied the minutiae, and I learned everything I could about the law. I mean I felt deeply inside that it was what I was born to do.
Mike:	And did your parents get over it?
Professor:	No. I always hoped that I would find some way to change their minds, but... they were inconsolable. My father never spoke to me again.
Mike:	If you had to do it all over again, would you make the same choices?

Professor:	What choice? The last thing I took away from the Yeshivas is... We can't run from who we are. Our destiny chooses us.

I have practically memorized every line from this scene because the thoughts from the dialog's last two lines have meant so much to me when I have struggled with tough decisions on staying in or leaving the game for good. No coach has ever been immune to those thoughts. Especially when dealing with late nights and weekends away from home, or having to justify playing time for an underachieving athlete to an unreasonable parent. But I ask you again, Remember...

Remember to go back to your earliest thoughts of why you wanted to become a coach. To help me remember, I recall a wise friend who once told me that he didn't believe in burnout. At the time I begged to differ, explaining to him it's often the price of knowing you are overworking, and under appreciated. He stopped me and said, "No, burnout occurs when we forget the focus."

As Petrovsky asked: "What choice? The last thing I took away from the Yeshivas is... We can't run from who we are. Our destiny chooses us."

Back to the opening thought of this open letter. You have or you will seriously contemplate getting out of coaching for good at some point. And unfortunately that thought or action will occur long before you have reached retirement age. I suggest you pause to remember. Remember the thoughts, the why's, and the dreams that urged your soul to get in the game.

Remember when that *why* was all you could think about, then remember this was what you *chose* to passionately pursue. So, "What choice? ... We can't run from who we are. Our destiny chooses us."

2.

Rich Hargitt - Head Coach Emmett HS - Emmett, ID

Trap and Belly RPOs

I started my coaching career at a small high school in East Central Illinois called Iroquois West High School. While there, I started learning the game of football from a Hall of Fame Football coach by the name of John Boma. John was in his last year of coaching and ran the Wing-T. When I took over my first program shortly afterwards in the same area of the state I kept many of the Wing-T principles that I learned and incorporated them into our own offense. We were an effective trap and belly team and I had my first 1,000 + yard back running the Down Belly as my feature run play. It is amusing for me to recount those days because now, 20 years later, we produced a 1,000 + yard running back and a 700+ yard rushing quarterback, and the belly was yet again one of the plays that helped us move the chains and succeed. The belly and trap are still great football plays and still great ways to move the ball. As we have done in The Surface To Air System so many times before, we have revolutionized and dressed these plays up and added an RPO to them and helped breath new life to them in our system. This chapter will talk briefly about the trap, as it was not a huge play for us but still helped the offense, but instead focus most heavily on the belly play, as it was a great play for us down the stretch as we mounted a playoff push.

The trap play has long been a great way to move the ball because of the angles it gives to the offensive linemen. We have featured both influence and non-influenced versions of this play. The main thing we did differently this year was that instead of asking our quarterback to check to the 3 technique we actually ran the play exclusively from an 11 personnel grouping and always featured a tight end that was attached or as a sniffer so that the defense would set their 3 technique where we could identify him early. In order to clean up the box we then featured a grass read to the call side and a simple RPO from our now screen package to the back door side of the play.

2-1

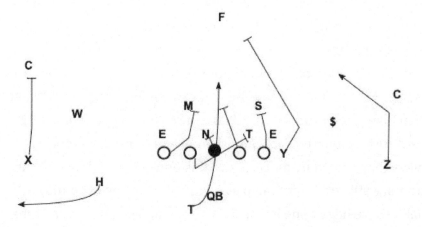

We taught the play as an unlocked RPO so that the quarterback could read it as a true triple option play. Another wrinkle we featured was to allow the back to swing to the two receiver side and lock the play while the quarterback had the option of running the trap or throwing the RPO to the grass.

2-2

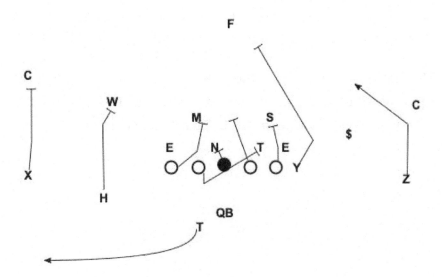

The benefit of adding this play back into our S2A world is that it gave us a great angle play that allowed our guards to be physical. We are the smallest school in our conference and the second smallest school in Idaho 4A and we need to generate angles to run the football. The trap play helped us to do just that this past fall.

Belly

The belly play is actually two different plays for us based upon whether it is executed to the tight end side or away from the tight end side. We really enjoy executing the play because of the natural ability of the quarterback to throw the ball without meshing with a running back. This empty RPO allows the quarterback to hold the ball as long as possible and make the defense honor and play a true 11-on-11 style of play. We execute distinctly different blocking schemes based upon whether or not the play is run to or away from the tight end.

The first way we like to run the belly is towards an open side with the running back set away from the tight end. This causes us to make a base call if we get a shade and a 5 technique.

2-3

If we had gotten a 3 technique we would make a cross block call, but we generally get an over front because of our tight end game and so therefore we get an easy iso style block to the open side of the formation. Our tackle will kick out the 5 techniques, while our guard and center work a combo up block on the shade technique and the backside linebacker. Our backside offensive linemen will execute a scoop technique and cut off all play side technique defenders and work to the second level of the defense. The ability to tag an RPO on the frontside of the run prevents the defense from running the invert defender back into the box to aide with the run play. We love the fact that we can hold the invert defender for an exceedingly long time and make a decision at the last moment. The quarterback's execution of the belly step, or horizontal initial release, aides in both the run action, distortion of the linebackers, and the read on the RPO.

The second main way to execute the belly play is to the tight end side of the formation. When we do this the play is often blocked as the G belly or down play from the traditional Wing-T playbook. This style of block will oftentimes lead to a cross block on the 3 technique side of the formation.

2-4

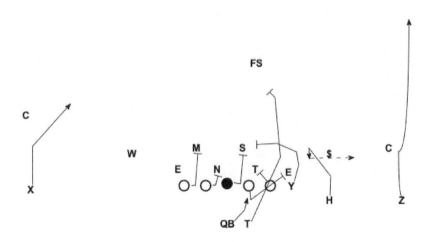

The tight end will fake a down block on an inside or 7 technique and then work to the first linebacker inside. If the defense plays with a 9 technique then the tight end will just block down onto the linebacker and allow for an easy kick out block by the pulling guard. The running back will run through the trap block and attack the play side linebacker to give the offense a numbers advantage. The defense will be forced to work the invert defender back into the box to equate numbers and thereby give the offense the opportunity to throw the RPO to the boundary.

Another interesting formational wrinkle is for the offense to align in a 3x1 unbalanced set. This set will allow the offense to force the defense to play a 3 technique to the four main surface side of the formation.

2-5

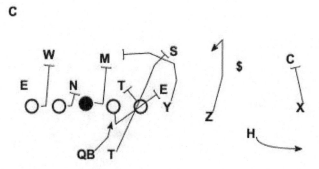

We will often see a 9 technique and trap all the way out with the pulling guard when we see odd front defenses.

2-6

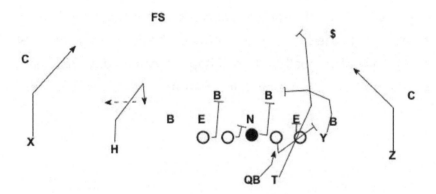

The defense is at a decided disadvantage and must move their front around very quickly to adjust to the natural numerical disadvantage they face. When we operate at a tempo pace that is faster, then we are able to manipulate the defense and we oftentimes get a misalignment on the box or on the perimeter. From here, we will get very easy run fits or an open receiver to throw the ball to on this type of play.

Conclusion

There are a large number of things to like about the Wing-T belly series. It was a good play for us 20 years ago when I started coaching football and it is a good play for us this fall when we improved our win total by two games and our rushing total by over 1100 yards. The advent and proliferation of RPOs have allowed the belly a new lease on life. The ability to put the quarterback into the run fit and take away the +1 advantage that the defense normally enjoys is a major factor in incorporating this run play. The fact that it allows the quarterback to carry the ball behind the running back is another quality reason to utilize the belly. This play is versatile and gives the play caller options to both the open and tight end side of the formation and marries up with an entire host of different RPO concepts to manipulate and distort the defense to the offense's advantage. The belly is alive and well in high school football and an untapped commodity that many coordinators will be rushing to incorporate in the years to come.

3.

Rich Hargitt - Head Coach Emmett HS - Emmett, ID

Power and Counter RPOs

The Power and Counter football plays have long been a staple of the game of football. These two plays have also been major contributors in the Wing-T style of play, I-Formation offense, and Spread offense. Each offensive evolution has put their own distinct wrinkles on these plays, but now the RPO has revolutionized the gap scheme plays like never before. These are "meat and potatoes" style runs that an offense can hang its hat on to win games and championships. When I took over a struggling Emmett program in 2018, we only rushed for 736 yards the entire season. In 2019, we made a commitment to incorporate more gap scheme runs into our package and increased our run total to over 1800 yards and won two extra games. In this chapter, we will delve into the world of power and counter gap scheme RPOs as they relate to a traditional Wing-T style of blocking schemes.

Power

The Power play has been a staple of offense for decades and has received a new and amazingly upgraded lease on life with the proliferation of RPOs. We have featured the power play as a change up play for our offense for years, but this past off-season we made the commitment to make a commitment to the power play. We felt that we needed to be more powerful and needed a character play that would allow our offense to play physical at the point of attack. We also had a pair of guards that we felt were tough kids that moved pretty well, and so it seemed the time was right to unleash Power as a central part of our attack on offenses.

We like to feature the power play from an 11 personnel set and utilize either the tight end in line or as a sniffer most of the time. Our base way to run the power play is to lock the scheme so that the backside tackle actually steps into the B gap and then kicks out the 5 technique defensive end.

3-1

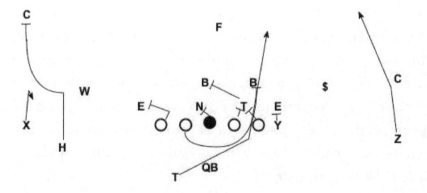

The center blocks back, on what is usually an A gap defender, and we double the 3 techniques and kick out the play side defensive end with our tight end. The last piece of the puzzle is for our backside guard top pull through the play side A gap and block the play side linebacker. If the double team on the 3 technique fills the A gap then the guard just adjusts his skip pull and works around the double team to the play side linebacker. The quarterback is able to work the Grass Slant Route to the front door side of the play or a Now Screen to the back door side should he feel there is a fall in player threatening the integrity of the play from either flank.

From time to time it serves our purpose to be able to read the power play as a true triple option RPO. When we decide to do this, we make a line call and the backside tackle will block the B gap and leave the backside 5 technique untouched and we will read that player.

3-2

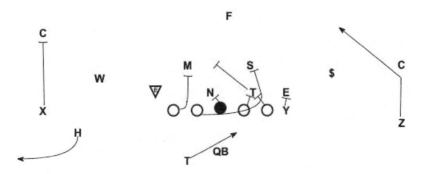

The ability to read the backside defense C gap player allows us greater flexibility in preventing the defense from playing line stunt games against our power play. This flexibility adds the quarterback run as yet another dimension that the defense must account for on any given snap.

Another useful technique that we have utilized this past season was the "same side" power technique. This means that the running back lines up on the same side of the formation that we will run Power towards.

3-3

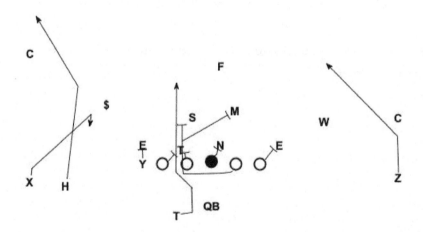

This is always run as a locked call and gives us tremendous options to distort the defense and prevent them from keying where the run will travel, based upon the location of the running back. This also enables the quarterback a better read on the RPO, since it is happening as a true back door read for the fall in player reactions.

We have really enjoyed utilizing a formation that we have played with for the last few years called Rock. The Rock Formation features the Y receiver, or tight end, aligned away from the other three receivers in the offense. We then execute Power towards the tight end side of the formation, while also having a three man surface to run our base RPO plays.

3-4

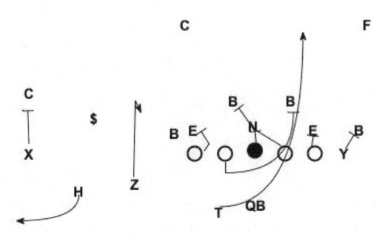

This diagram is outlined versus an Odd Front defense; in this case a standard Okie or 3-4 defense. Our play side tackle will make an Odd Call and then attempt to kick out the head up defensive player while the tight end does the exact same thing. We double the nose tackle and pull our backside guard around to block the play side linebacker. If the play side tackle misses his block and is forced to block down, then the backside guard will pull around and fit accordingly. It is our opinion that the power play can easily be fit to run effectively against both an even and an odd front with this simple and easy-to-teach line call adjustment.

Another formation quirk we have utilized this fall is the Elk Formation, which features the tight end as a split back.

3-5

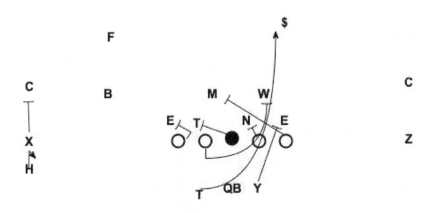

This alignment allows us to get a better kick out angle against the play side defensive end. As you will note, this diagram is against an under front and will be a slightly different adjustment scenario for the offense. This Elk Formation is a simple way to get the angles we want while also making the defense prepare for, and be cognizant of, the potential for a split zone RPO and not being able to sell out fully to stop the power play. In essence, the Elk Formation is basically camouflage to protect the power play, as it is a set from which we normally run inside zone and makes the defense guess instead of being able to use formational recognition against us.

As noted above, we must make adjustments when we see an under front. The Elk Formation is certainly one way to help alleviate the under front stressors, and even more adjustments have been utilized. An under front is a front where the defense puts the 3 technique away from the tight end side and the shade defensive tackle to the tight end side of the formation. One simple solution we have made is to make an Odd Call and attack this even front under defense as if it is actually an odd front structure.

3-6

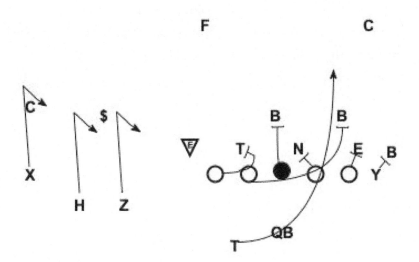

The nose tackle gets double teamed and we kick out the play side defensive end and walk up linebackers. The really tough block is to take care of the backside 3 technique tackle. If we are unable to scoop block him, we simply cut block him and run the ball away from the defender. This has proven itself to be a solution that is very useful versus an under front, but we have also had to be willing to utilize the power play's cousin, the counter.

Counter

In S2A, it is our opinion that if you want to be a good power team you must also be a good counter team. The counter is really the power and the power is really the counter; they are symbiotic plays that are part of the overall gap scheme that makes the Surface to Air System an effective physical run system.

If our quarterbacks are outnumbered, they are allowed to kill a power play and move to a counter play instead. There are certain teams and certain personnel groups where this is an automatic adjustment. For example, if we see a team play an under front to the tight end side, then we will allow the quarterback to kill or audible to a same side GY (named after the guard and Y receiver) counter play that will become a same side run.

3-7

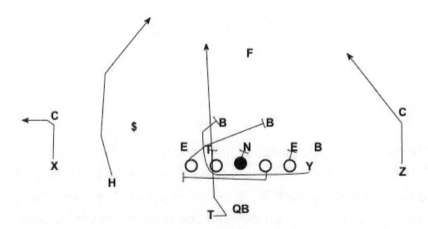

We are now able to get the double team on the 3 technique that we wish to create, a down block on the shaded nose tackle, kick out on the defensive end, and a lead through on the play side linebacker. This is essentially a way to run the power play but off of a counter style action. We actually do not practice power without also getting reps practicing counter. We feel they are built for the same purpose and from the same platform.

Another great counter play is the GT (named for the guard and tackle) Counter that also allows us to run the power towards the shade tackle tight end side of the formation, but again off of a counter action.

3-8

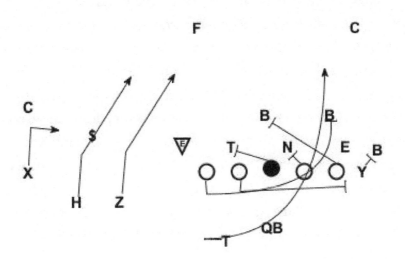

We instruct our tight end to always block the first player outside the defensive end on counter trey (the generic name for GT is counter trey). From this, we get down blocks on the 3 technique and shade tackles and a kick out block on the play side defensive end and a pull around for the play side linebacker. This allows us to block the power play again from yet another counter run action.

Conclusion

We are a big fan of running the power play in the modern game of football because it is a character play that allows us to be a physical run team. We love that power is a double team at the point of attack and a kick out and pull around to the second level and we feel that counter is really the same play. The power, GY counter, and GT counter are all really the same play and we feel that the call to be made is basically determined by what the defense does to combat our angles and grass. The ability to RPO these plays means that we no longer have to account for defensive fall in players or secondary coverage rotation to stop or gap runs. Our quarterbacks can simply throw these players out of the box. This leaves the defense with one answer - to use their box players to alter the angles that we prefer to utilize to run the football. The ability to block the power three different ways allows us to negate these adjustments and dictate how and where we can run the football. Therefore, the RPOs handle secondary measures to stop the play. Our ability to kill and alter schemes at the line of scrimmage allows our quarterback to keep the numbers and angles in our favor. This modern evolution of power and counter from the Surface to Air System has made this scheme a "go-to" option in our offense for years to come.

4.

Rich Hargitt - Head Coach Emmett HS - Emmett, ID

Buck sweep RPOs

In 2018 I took over the Emmett football program and the players were not yet strong enough to run the ball. Therefore, we utilized our strengths, which allowed our team to break the school passing records and stay competitive. This past year, my second at the head of the program, we made the decision that we would play physical football. We were still a traditional Inside and Outside Zone team, but incorporated Power and Counter into our DNA as well. A few games into the season we realized that teams were selling out to stop our outside zone run plays, which meant we had to pivot and make another addition. This time the buck sweep was added to the package. I had experience with this Wing-T "blast from the past" and had run it sparingly a few years ago. But now, it was made a huge part of our offense and became a fully integrated RPO package to help us increase our run physicality and improve our yards per rush and win totals in 2019.

Buck sweep has long been a part of wing-t offenses and has helped many teams to play competitive football. The first thing to note about buck sweep is that it is not as much a sweep as it is power, one gap wider. We have found that this play is versatile and allows us an outside power type play that prevents defenses from taking away our interior runs, and also prevents them from utilizing anti-outside countermeasures. This play has shown itself to be effective as both a running back and a quarterback based run play.

Base Buck sweep RPOs

In our offense, the base buck sweep play is executed from an 11 personnel set. We can use both a sniffer as well as an in-line tight end to execute the play, but we prefer the angle of the attached tight end more than the sniffer. Our base rule for the tight end is that he blocks the first player inside of him. This means if the defensive end is head up or outside then our tight end will block down and we will trap that player. We will only block first level with the tight end if there is a player in the C gap or lined up head up on the offensive tackle. We have our tackle block down and our play side guard pulls and kicks out the first defender outside the tight end.

4-1

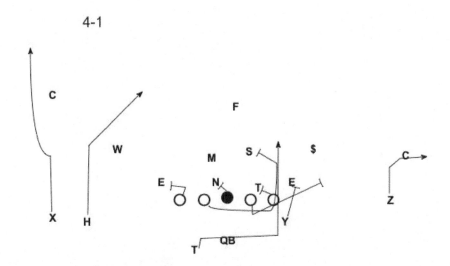

The center blocks the most dangerous A gap threat, preferably a down block, and the backside guard pulls and leads through the hole underneath the first guard's kick out block. We generally lock the backside tackle on the backside defensive end, but we are able to read the end from time to time. We will oftentimes allow the front door receiver a route that takes coverage away from the run lane and execute a man-beating and deeper level RPO on the back door side. We have found that we can throw deeper and more explosive RPOs off of buck sweep thanks to the fact that the timing is better for holding the mesh longer and elongating the distance the receiver can travel before the guards engaged. This adds to the lethality of the RPO version of the buck sweep. We also love to run the buck sweep from the Rock Formation.

4-2

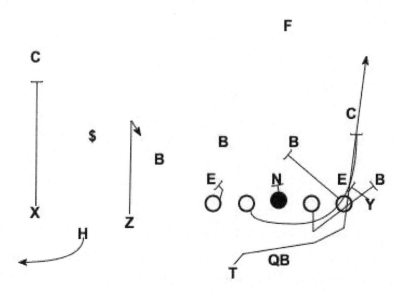

This formation forces the defense to commit a contain and force player to the short or tight end side of the formation and allows us to generally kick out the contain player and run underneath the force and coverage player. We generally feel that buck sweep is better the faster we get down hill, and this set lends itself to that eventuality. This is the sort of play we can read, but generally leave the play locked and force the defense to either hold players on the backside of the play and waste them or allow them to read and run to open up a late RPO throw for the quarterback.

It is also helpful to put two receivers on the front door side of the buck sweep play and be able to move the invert player on the front door side with an RPO.

4-3

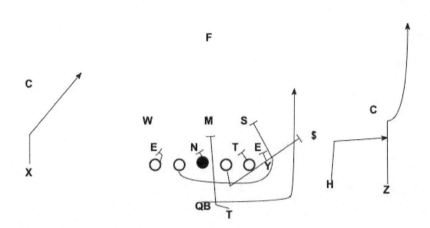

This type of formational tweak allows us to keep the strong safety out of the box and if he attempts to fall back in and support the run then he will be read and thrown off by the quarterback. The ability to move the slot receiver to both the front and back door is a huge advantage for the offense and gives us increased flexibility in distorting the defense.

Alterations to Buck sweep RPOs

We feel that minor alterations to the basic buck sweep can yield huge dividends. Some of these changes are incredibly small, yet aide in making the play more efficient and devastating. One such advantage is to set the back to the tight end side on the rock formation.

4-4

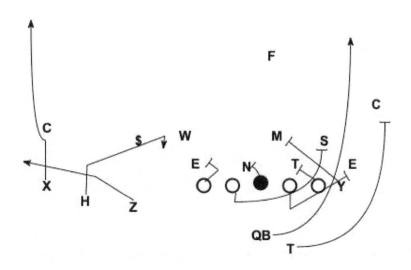

This set allows us to run counter back to the trips side or to run the quarterback belly to the tight end side so the defense must account for both of these sorts of blocking scheme adjustments. However, we discovered that the running back can be sent on a lead call and sent around the tight end side to facilitate the edge of the nub or tight end side run. We often get a double team on the contain player and sometimes we end up getting the running back all the way to the force player. This provides extra blocking at the point of attack, but also influences the contain player to widen when he sees the running back arc outside and facilitates the trap block by the pulling guard. The quarterback run also gives the offense an 11-on-11 opportunities and the RPO can and has been thrown pre-snap by the quarterback to keep the defense stalled on the backside of the play.

Another interesting tweak is to motion the Z receiver into the formation and have him crack the invert player.

4-5

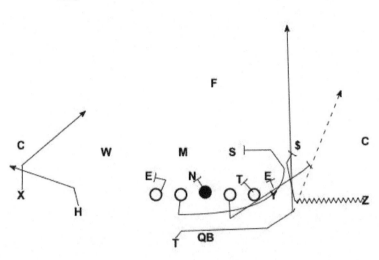

The Z receiver has sometimes blocked the invert down and we have pulled all the way to the corner, yet other times we have ended up double teaming that player. The advantage is that our guards are able to come around the edge and work more downhill and the running back has been able to bounce the play and get wider runs. We have also utilized the H receiver as a motion man and actually handed him the football and made him the buck sweep player.

4-6

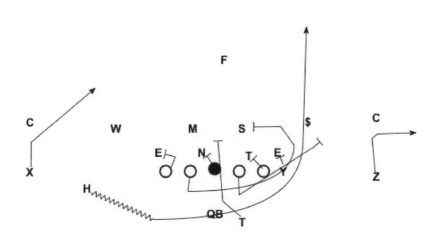

This gives us an advantage because we are able to send the running back into the play side A gap and stop any double A gap blitzes that the defense may have devised in an attempt to stop the buck sweep. This is a useful and very inexpensive countermeasure to stop teams that attempt to blitz the buck sweep from inside out in an effort to stall the play. It also gets us a new ball carrier to the ball and provides a scissors action in the backfield that keeps linebackers feet very heavy. The motion options, whether as a ball carrier or a blocker, are numerous and a wrinkle that can really dress the buck sweep play up quite effectively.

Unbalanced Buck sweep RPOs

An amazingly simple and immensely effective play for us this fall was unbalanced quarterback buck sweep runs. We actually had a game that we won this fall and ran just shy of 400 yards rushing in the game. Our principal run play in that contest was the unbalanced quarterback buck sweep play. This play lets the offense play 11 on 11. The team we faced played cover 0 (man coverage with no safety over the top) and this play allowed us to equate numbers and then gain a numerical advantage at the point of attack.

The first way that we ran the unbalanced buck sweep was with the cross block action by the running back.

4-7

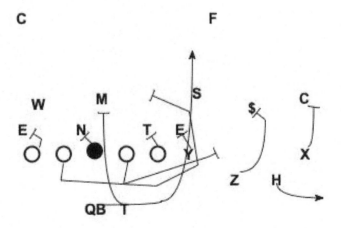

This style of blocking allowed us to take away the A gap stunts teams like to use and provide "eye candy" by sending our running back away from the eventual destination of the play. The quarterback was able to ride the running back and then work to the perimeter while keeping his eyes on the RPO down to the very last second. It is very difficult for the defense to handle this because their fall-in players cannot risk leaving their receivers until the very last second since the quarterback can hold the ball for so long. The quarterback is able to fake the throw or run and to keep the defense guessing long into the progression.

Another easy blocking adjustment is to line up unbalanced and then send the running back on a lead path to guide the quarterback to the unbalanced flank of the defense.

4-8

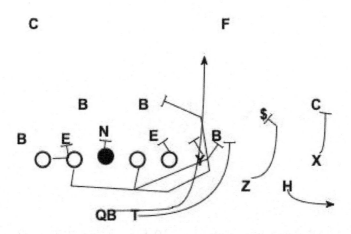

This forces the contain player to widen for fear of being reached and then sets him up for a kick out block. If the contain player does not widen then we would simply call an outside zone play to the quarterback and lead him around the flank with the running back. Once again, the RPO prevents any defensive rotations, stunts, or fall-ins in order to get extra hats to the run box. These formations are very easy for us to signal and the flexibility of the Surface to Air System lets us easily integrate these plays and formations into a drive with only minimal signaling.

Conclusion

I have long been a fan of the Wing-T offense because it creates conflicts for the defense to solve that are not easy to overcome. The wing-t style of play has fallen out of favor with the modern offensive coach because it is seen as stale and unadventurous. However, the advent of RPOs, unbalanced sets, motion principles, and formational variations have added a great deal of spice to these plays and makes them variable and incredibly useful instruments to the modern spread offense play caller. The RPO has given these less adventurous wing-t plays a new lot on life and returned them to the pantheon of effective and physical running plays as part of the Surface to Air System.

5.

Eric Solbakken - Assistant Coach - Lake Stevens HS Lake Stevens, WA

Incorporating a Simple Run Game Language

Introduction

"The deepest back". A reply text message I received from a high level linebacker coach. I asked him, "What would be your read against these looks?" Needles to say, his encouragement by just simply interacting with me led to this content.

After studying a variety of offenses and trying to figure out how to put the run game into different series and why they would be grouped into said series, we finally arrived at grouping the series by numbers. This is not new, but stolen from various people that are smarter than me. We wanted to find a way to run both gap and zone blocking schemes, but not introduce them as two totally separate blocking schemes. Furthermore, these two schemes carry components that compliment each other in a significant way. As we ventured into last year's season (2018) we studied the Nevada offense and various offenses around the country that ran both zone and gap. While pairing the fact that most linebacker coaches read the deepest back in the backfield, we also looked at what made a backfield mesh. We came up with the following:

1. The alignment of the ball carrier
2. The path of the ball carrier as it relates to the blockers in front
3. The footwork of the ball carrier
4. The footwork of the player initiating the mesh

As we considered all of these factors, we came up with a double digit numbering system to decipher what each running play would be called.

Chart 5-1

Series	Inside Ball Carrier	Outside Ball Carrier	Visual	Run Scheme
10	QB	TB		Zone
20	TB	QB		Zone
30	QB	S		Zone
40	TB/QB	TB/QB		Zone
50	TB/QB	TB/QB		Gap

We poured over the language that people have used across football during the modern times, as well as how the run game was called in previous decades. We see offensive football as having a number of elements to it, and being able to hear a play call and know if it is a run or a pass based on a number was key for us. When the run game is your identity, it becomes mission critical to make sure that our players do not have to try and decode what words are to get to the run schemes or tracks. Systems that we have poured over from around our area have typically used redundant numbering systems. For example, naming a play "24 blast" becomes redundant from a play calling perspective when the 4 means blast in the first place. So, the question becomes, "Why call it 24 blast?" Searching far and wide for how we were going to teach this, we arrived at the Single Wing system ran by Rich Darlington of Enterprise High School in Alabama. Darlington's Single Wing system brought elite simplicity to the run game, and gave the words after the numbers meaning for us. Each of these run series is also tied to either a zone or a gap scheme. The Single Wing allowed us to piece together a system that produced multiple backfield alignments, and different run schemes so that the linemen understood the effects that each backfield action would produce. The words that come after the number in a play call are tags for the Hybrid back, the Tailback, and the Tackle. No longer would "24 Blast" mean "24 Blast-Blast" With such a small detail, we had a way to teach the run game to our kids in a short amount of time. With just two numbers and a tag, we had our:

1. Backfield alignment
2. Run Scheme
3. Track of ball carrier

4. Specific way we would handle the Defensive End/Force Player

The following sections will detail a bit of history detailing how we arrived with these series as the core of our run game.

The 10 Series

Our play calling system allows us to create tendencies for the opponent. The benefit we get on this element of our offense is that it allows the quarterback's footwork to stay consistent within each run series.

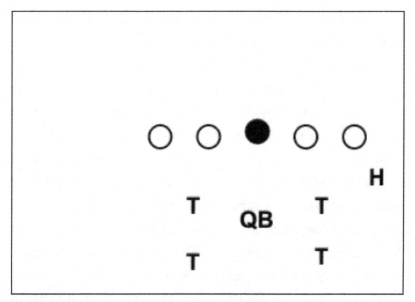

Diagram 5-1

Diagram 5-1 shows the different alignments the tailback can get in as it relates to the quarterback's hip. As a base alignment, the 10 Series aligns the tailback away from the call and with his heals at the quarterback's toes. One of the growing pains we went through last season was the question of "where do we align the back width wise?" As we messed around with this, we found that some of our tailbacks needed be lined up on the outside leg of the guard, some needed to be aligned in the B-Gap, some needed to be aligned on the inside leg of the tackle, and on rare occasions, we aligned him over head up over the tackle. The historical term for the run series you may see out of this backfield alignment would be the "inverted veer" series.

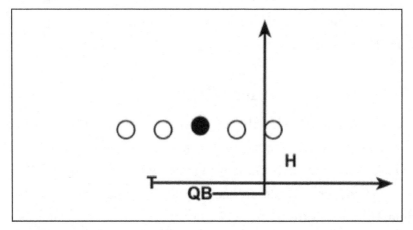

Diagram 5-2

The base run for the tailback in this series is outside zone. (Diagram 5-2) The track for the tailback on this run is the inside leg of the very most outside pass catcher detached from the line of scrimmage. If the ball is being run to an unbalanced or nub side, we would track the top of the numbers. In most inverted veer looks the quarterback would be asked to drop step to get to his mesh point, due to the back being in a toe to heal relationship to the back. Declaring the alignment for the back in terms of his depth has allowed for the quarterback's footwork much easier to learn.

The next critical element of this series is that it lives in the zone family. As we have taught our players, when the ball is snapped and handed off, if the three inside linemen are blocking in the direction where the ball is going, then we are running a play in the zone family. Therefore, whenever something in the ten series is called, they can expect flow to the side that the ball is going. As this series is based off the QB running the ball, leaving the end unblocked each play and giving the QB a read that he can clearly see in the heat of the moment will greatly increase our chances of generating a win on that particular down, or an explosive play of 12 yards or more.

The 20 Series

This last fall, we installed this series first, as we were still unsure what was going to fit our players' needs. In the 20 series, the tailback aligns in a hip alignment next to the QB, just like in the 10 series. However, the difference lies in the relationship of the tailback's toes to the QB's heels. In the 20 Series, the tailback's toes are directly aligned at the quarterback's heels as a default. As shown in the 10 series, the alignment from the default will vary based off of player skill. Width wise, this alignment will start out as a default with the tailback aligning over the outside leg of the offensive guard. The largest difference from the 10 series is that the tailback will have extra yards to play with depth wise in order to hit the line of scrimmage as the holes are opening up. In the 20 series, the tailback will align also, away from the call. The primary run that the series is based out of is inside zone, or 1 and 2. The quarterback will turn and faced the unblocked defensive end and keep him home as the tailback chases the inside leg of the guard in our inside zone look.

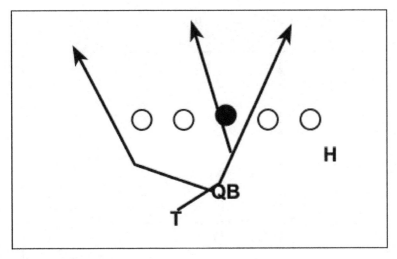

Diagram 5-3

As we established inside zone out of this look, teams usually started to call out what the play was based off of the backs alignment, and we accepted this. The same tags could be called out of the 20 series that we called in the 10 series.

30 Series

The 30 Series was one of our favorite ways to attack the flank a different way than what we considered our identity. Our base way of attacking the flank was attaching fast screens and quick game concepts to our runs. The 30 series was the well-known fly sweep series, and completely an offshoot of our Rick Darlington single wing days. The 30 Series presented another way for one of our dynamic runners to get the ball in space in a different way other our RPO's. This series presented a way for our quarterback to get the ball in his hands in a downhill running manner. Similar to the 10 Series, the QB will stick the ball out in front of him on the snap while our slot back runs in front of him in a fly sweep path. The diagram looks identical to the 10 series path that the tailback takes on his 10 series outside zone runs.

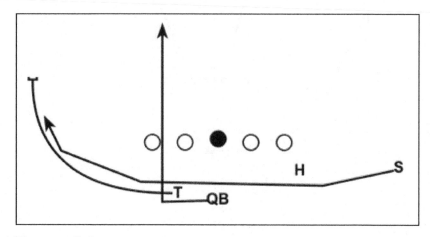

Diagram 5-4

To further provide headaches to the defense we added different tailback alignments to this look, as well as every tag found in our running game. The base alignment that the tailback would get in is the 10 series alignment. Naming these series the way that we did provided an accelerated way for our players to align in specific areas on the fly. For example, our default in any 30 Series run was for the tailback to get into a 10 Series alignment and be the lead blocker for the fly back. Toward the end of last season, teams understood this and started to rotate coverage toward the back if they knew the 30 Series was coming. We began to establish a running game out of our 50 Series (Pistol alignment), aligning the tailback in a 50 Series alignment for a majority of many games to offset any tendency we had when we still wanted to get the edge. Any and all inside runs for us were still available to us in this series.

40 Series

As we aimed for providing some variety in our backfield sets, we really started to enjoy Pistol for the obvious reason that most people do, it gave us a downhill running look. In addition to having pistol as our run series, we lined up in pistol before every play in order to hide the alignment of our back. In our 40 series, we based our running game out of zone.

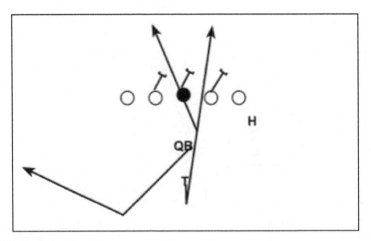

Diagram 5-5

Both our quarterback and tailback would open up to the call side. As the ball was snapped, the tailback would assume the track of the play called. After the QB handed off the ball, he would either boot outside off the tackle box to strengthen our naked series passing game, or he would post up in the center of the pocket for a drop back play action pass look. Most people would look at the 40 series and identify it as associated with a pro-style offense. We believed that this was something that was necessary to carry in our offense.

<u>50 Series</u>

Our fifth and final base series that is a part of our running game is our pistol zone read series that was highly influenced from Chris Ault. When we started the year, we assumed that we would be a 20 Series running team. As the year went on we identified a few different running backs that we could feature. Due to injuries and players developing, we found that one of our running backs, who will be one of the feature backs for this upcoming team, ran the best out of the pistol.

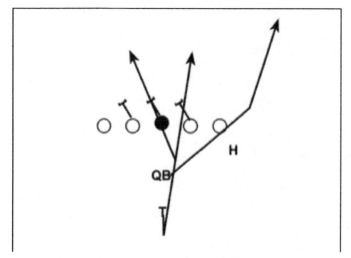

Figure 5-6

The base running scheme that the 50 Series is housed in the gap running scheme. This series made it easy for us to read the defensive end and get downhill with the ball carrier without having to be under center, in what would be a typical flexbone look for most veer teams that live under center.

Conclusion

These run series are all stolen. Most people might read this and say, "yeah Eric, everyone runs that." Those who say those things are right. What this comes down to is getting down to my philosophy as a play caller, trial and error, and the most important ingredient to execution of all, players. Rich Hargitt, Dub Maddox, Darrell Bevell, Brian Schottenheimer, Dan Gonzalez, and Rich Darlington are some of my biggest influences to date. I am grateful for the many people that I have met along my 10 year football journey. Please reach out to me if you have any questions about this chapter on Twitter @CoachSolbakken, or via email: esolbakken23@gmail.com.

6.

Steve Kirk - Head Coach Argenta-Oreana HS - Argenta, IL

Base Screen Game

The screen game is an integral part of any offensive system. Whether it is the Wing-T or Empty, there are many yards to be had through the screen game. The screen game is a great way to get your best players the ball and allow them to make plays in space. There are multitudes of ways to do this, whether it be through utilizing a basic running back under screen, or utilizing the wide receiver screens made popular in today's spread offenses, such as the tunnel and jailbreak screens. Additionally, as a general rule screens are low risk plays with high reward potential. You can watch any football game and see big plays on screens in just about every game you watch.

The advent of modern defenses has found ways to control and sometimes stymie spread offenses. Offensive coordinators must always be thinking one step ahead of today's defensive coordinators. Gone are the days of defenses sitting in one front and one coverage for the duration of the game and allowing offenses to dictate the game. Modern defenses will play match coverages, and have the ability to blitz from anywhere on the field. Today's offensive coordinators must have an answer and be able to take advantage of the weaknesses of these fronts and coverages. In our screen package we try to have an answer for anything a defense can throw at us in any given situation through the screen game.

We believe in having screens that beat man coverage and screens that beat zone coverages. Moreover, we want to give our quarterback options in our screen game. Rarely, if ever do we call a screen without something else being attached to that screen. Today's offenses commonly refer to this as a pass-screen option (PSO). In the PSO, one side of the formation will be given a route concept to run and the other side of the formation will be given the screen. The quarterback will read the route combination first, and if he likes the passing route combination he will throw it to that side. If he doesn't like it or it is not open, then he will come back to the other side of the formation and run the called screen. I believe this gives our quarterback a ton of confidence, and gives our offense a lot of flexibility in getting the ball to the correct place.

Lastly, with as much advanced scouting that goes on in today's game, defenses are better prepared than ever before. They know what you like to run out of certain formations as well as your down and distance tendencies. Offenses must know that through their own self-scout protocol, and be able to counter what the defense is expecting. We like to do this by running our same screens multiple different ways. We will run our favorite screens with a different formation or motion depending on the week and what films the opposing team has on us. This not only is a different look for the defense, but it helps to keep our screens fresh for our players.

TB UNDER SCREEN

The under screen is one of the most utilized screens in today's offenses. It can be run out of many formations, and be dressed up in just about every way imaginable. This screen can be run from every personnel grouping and can be run with motions and shifts to make the play go. It is certainly one of the most versatile plays in football today.

As previously stated, we prefer to run our TB under screen as a pass-screen option (PSO). When we install this play we install it from a trips formation. The pass concept that we like to utilize opposite the screen is the stick concept. In the stick concept the Y will run the stick route, the F will run a bubble and the Z will run the post. We ask our Y to run five steps and find the open area between the Mike and the Sam. He has the option to break out if the Mike is fitting his route. The receiver to the side of the screen (X) will push-crack the safety in any two-high coverage. If the coverage is a one-high structure, then the X will attempt to run off the corner before stalk blocking him.

The offensive line will make this play go. The PST will pass set and invite the DE up the field. The PSG and C will be the two offensive linemen that will release on the screen. They will pass set opposite the call and count for two-seconds and then go. The PSG will release to what we call the sidewalk. This is a general term we use to describe the area between the numbers and the sideline.

This helps his angle of departure. The C will release and block the defender in the alley. This is the term we use to describe the area between the numbers and the hash. Again, by describing it with these terms it helps to get them on the correct angle of departure. The BSG and BST will slide to the call and block man on.

The TB is responsible for the timing of the play on the screen side. He cannot leave too early, otherwise he risks not having his lineman in front of him once he catches the football. On the snap of the ball, the TB will step into the B gap and check for a Will linebacker blitz or the blitz of a rolled down safety. If one of those two individuals blitzes, he is responsible for stopping the charge of the blitz before releasing.

The TB will count one-second and then go, before releasing to approximately four yards outside the PST original alignment. It is absolutely imperative that the TB find a clear throwing lane for the QB to deal him the ball. We do not want the throw to sail over the head of a defensive lineman because the ball is in the air too long, and risk getting it picked off and run the other way for a defensive score.

The QBs job on this play is two-fold. First, he will read the drop of the Mike linebacker. If the Mike linebacker does not fit the stick route he will catch, turn, and deal the ball to the Y immediately. If the Mike fits the stick, or he does not like the concept because it is not a clear picture in his mind, he will then take a three-step drop getting as much depth as he can. He will throw the screen to the TB who has given him an open window to throw the ball. The ball should be thrown on a line, but should be easily catchable.

The diagrams listed below show the play against both a one high and two high defensive structure.

TB UNDER SCREEN VS. 1 HIGH

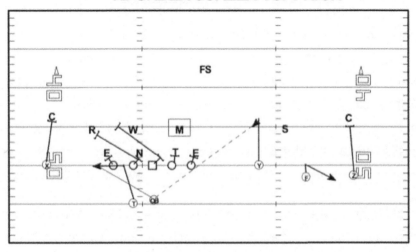

TB UNDER SCREEN VS. 2 HIGH

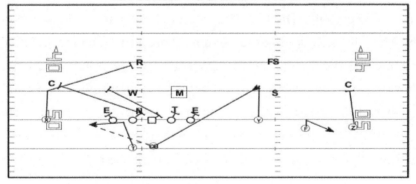

Variations of the TB Under Screen

It is my belief that you should have a few different looks for the defense while running the same play. We feel with the great job defensive coordinators are doing these days, we need multiple ways to run the same screen to keep defenses off balance. This keeps it simple for our kids, but gives defenses one more thing to prepare for, or gives them something they have not seen before.

This screen matches up well out of our two-back formation. We will send a back out in motion and build our pass concept that way. You can really build any concept you want to the motion side. We will throw the ball out to the motion man on a swing quite often. Additionally, we will run a three man snag concept to that side as well. Of course, you can just keep the stick concept on and run it the exact same way as described above. The beauty of this is you can build it pretty much any way you want and it stays the same for everyone involved with just a few minor tweaks.

Another great way to run this play is from a 2x2 set. When we run this play from this set we like to attach the play with our shallow concept. Our F will run the shallow and Y will run the dig. Our Z will run a post and X will run a go. The TB will run his normal under screen path. The QB rules do not change at all. He will read the Mike. If the Mike takes a deep pass drop then the QB will deal the ball to the F on the shallow route. If the Mike takes the shallow, the QB will then reset his feet and throw the screen. Again, nothing has changed for anyone, except we added a route concept that we run all the time anyway. The reads stay the same for the QB and the scheme stays the same for the offensive line.

TB UNDER SCREEN W/ SWING

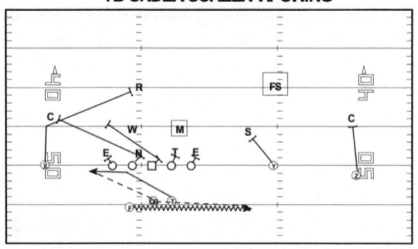

TB UNDER SCREEN/SHALLOW

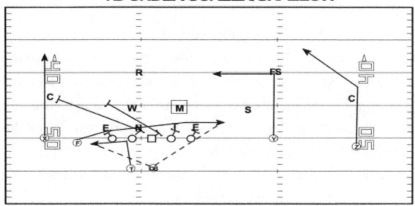

TB SWING SCREEN

The TB swing screen is a great way to get your TB out in space where he can display his natural talents effectively. This is a screen that is a simple and effective way for you to get your TB on the flank of the defense quickly and with blockers in front. I like to think of this play as the spread offenses version of the Flex-bone rocket toss.

This play is another one of our PSO concepts. We will install this out of a two back formation in summer camp, but it can be run from many different formations. We will discuss this play like we are installing it from a 2x1 set.

TB SWING SCREEN

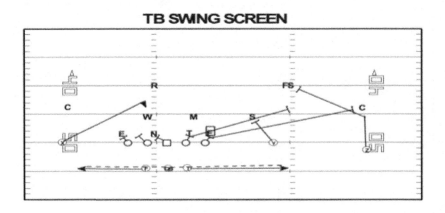

The Y and Z will line up together with the X on the other side of the formation. The TB will be aligned with the Y and Z next to the QB and the F will be aligned on the other side of the QB. The Z will be responsible for the push-crack against any two-high structure and stalk block against any one-high structure. The Y will be responsible for the defender on or inside of him. This player is usually the Sam backer. We will discuss the X and F responsibility a little later as they will be on the concept side.

The PST and PSG will be the two players who release on this play. They will block man on for a one-second count and then go. It is absolutely imperative that these players release behind the defender as to not cross their face. If they cross the face of the DL, it will almost certainly alert the DL that a screen is coming. The PST will be responsible for the sidewalk and the PSG will be responsible for the alley. The C, BSG, BST will slide away from the call. The TB will execute a five-step swing route and expect the ball. Depending on the type of athlete you have at TB, you may need him to take a false step before leaving to not outrun his blockers. The F and X will execute a two-man snag concept. The X will run to the B gap at eight yards and once he crosses the flat defender he will show his numbers to the QB. The F will execute a three-step swing route and expect the ball. He should end up at the bottom of the numbers.

The QB will take a three-step drop and read the screen side DE. If the DE continues to rush the passer then the screen will be thrown on the third step. If the DE peels and runs with the back to the point where we cannot get the screen off, then the QB will flip his hips and work the concept side, which in this case is the two-man snag side. The screen is the first read in this case, so we want to throw that first unless it is not there or the QB does not feel comfortable pitching it out on the perimeter.

Variations of the TB Swing Screen

As you can probably imagine, there are a multitude of variations to this play. The possibilities are endless when you start to build in your favorite pass or screen concepts in concert with the swing screen. One of my favorite ways to run it is out of a trips set. I prefer to run the screen away from the trips side and to have the X crack the first linebacker in the box. This is commonly referred to as a crack screen. The offensive line rules do not change, with the PST taking the sidewalk which would be the corner, and the PSG taking the next off-color jersey which may be a safety or inside linebacker, depending on who shows up in the alley. The QB will still read the end and throw off of him. The coach can build whatever concept he wants to the trips side, however I prefer a tunnel screen.

In our tunnel screen, the Z would stalk block the corner and the Y would block the next man from the sideline, which is almost always the Sam or Safety in man free coverage. Our F would show bubble for timing purposes before breaking inside to receive the tunnel screen. If you prefer your outside receiver being the tunnel guy, you can easily block out with the F and let the Z be the tunnel runner. The same two offensive linemen release with the PST having the third defender from the sideline and the PSG taking the first defender in the box, which is usually the Mike.

TB SWING SCREEN W TUNNEL SCREEN

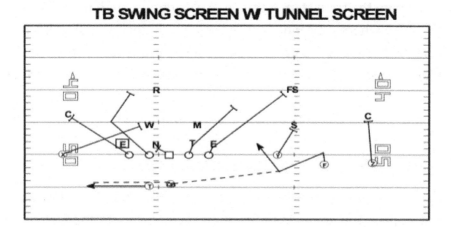

TUNNEL SCREEN

The tunnel screen is a great way to get one of your top playmakers the ball in space. It is also a great blitz beater call in which you have the opportunity to turn the play into a touchdown. The tunnel screen is a relatively easy play to install and has the opportunity to gain big chunks of yardage. This play has been, and still is, a staple of any spread offense.

This play is another one of our PSO concepts. We will run this play from a trips formation and attach some kind of pass concept to the single receiver side. We will install it using the 2 man snag concept discussed previously.

TUNNEL SCREEN

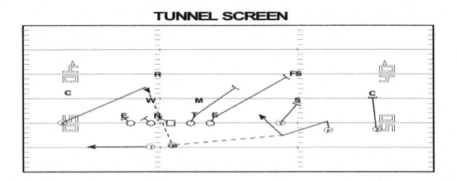

As stated above, the two-man snag consists of the X receiver running a snag route, and the TB running a swing route. The tunnel screen is the same screen we attached to our swing screen variation. The Z would stalk block the corner and the Y would block the next man inside which is almost always the Sam or Safety in man free coverage. Our F would show bubble for timing purposes, before breaking inside to receive the tunnel screen. The two offensive lineman releasing are the PST and PSG, with the PST having the third defender from the sideline and the PSG taking the first defender in the box, which is usually the Mike.

The QB will read the concept side first. He will take a three-step drop and throw the snag on rhythm. If the snag is not there, he will reset his feet and throw the tunnel screen to the F receiver.

As with most of the other plays discussed, this can be built in a number of different ways. It would be very easy to change the front side route combination or run the play out of 2x2 and have a two or three man route combination going on with a tunnel screen. It is a very versatile play that I believe will garner good results in any system.

JAILBREAK SCREEN

The jailbreak screen is the only screen we have that does not have a PSO attached to it. The reason for this is that we are a big GT counter team and we like to run this screen off of our counter action and try to get the numbers in our favor that way. There is no reason you could not make this play part of your PSO package if you so desired, we just choose to run it this way based on our system.

Our jailbreak screen is run from a 2x2 set. The Z will be the jailbreak runner. His rules are fast hands, fast feet and retrace to the QB. The Y will push vertical and then block the corner. The F and X are not involved in the play and will simply execute a bubble screen look to try and occupy the corner and safety to that side.

The PSG and PST will pull like they would on GT counter and block the people they would normally be responsible for on that play, which are the DE and LB. The C will be fast and flat and he will block the second guy from the sideline, which is usually the Sam. The BSG will be fast and flat for the first guy in the box, which is the Mike. If the Mike chases the counter action the BSG will climb to the FS. The BST will be fast and flat for the second guy in the box, which is the Will in most cases. Again, if the Will leaves to make a play on the TB then he can climb to the third level. The QBs job is to make a really good fake to the TB who is running his counter path. The QB will disengage from the TB belly and retreat two or three steps and deliver the ball to the Z on the screen.

JAILBREAK SCREEN

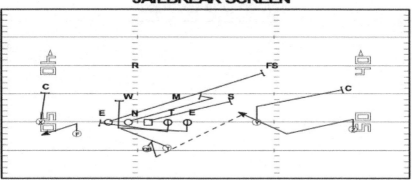

Practicing Your Screen Game

I believe to be good at screens you must place an emphasis on them. We practice our screens daily through our screen drill. We dedicate two 5 minute periods per day to our screen drill. This allows us to get about 20 reps of the screen of the day during the drill. Moreover, we will sprinkle our screens into our skelly and team periods to get about 25 reps at a particular screen per day.

When we set up our screen drill we will place stand up dummies in place where defenders that will need to be blocked by our receivers and releasing linemen. For example, we will place a dummy as a half field safety, corner, and inside linebacker. Our first group will come up and execute the called screen and finish in the end zone. One QB will throw the screen and another QB will execute the pass option off of the screen. Coaches are responsible for making sure that each person in their position group ran the play correctly. They must coach on the run because this is a fast paced drill. Once the first unit completes their rep, the second unit will snap the ball and do the same thing. We usually have four full units going. Any extra kids will have to rotate in. We will get three reps each on the screen, then run the same screen the opposite way.

Screen Drill Example

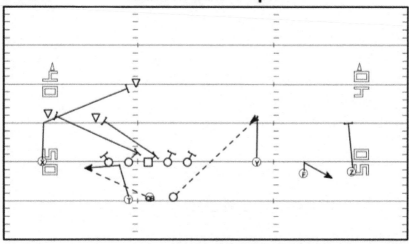

7.

Brian Brady - Head Coach Carson Graham Secondary North Vancouver, Canada

Protecting Your Best Runs with RPOs

Perhaps the most beneficial aspect of incorporating Run Pass Options into our offense has been our increased ability to protect our best run plays. Our most explosive play over the past five years has been our Dart run with quick and intermediate Air Raid passing concepts attached. The Dart gives the quarterback a clean zone read on the defensive end and, if he is an athlete, we have another way to get the ball to a playmaker.

This chapter will overview how we have attached RPOs to our Dart play while adapting to the defense's squeeze and scrape by attaching a sniffer tight end and attaching first and second level passing concepts. This has not only protected our zone read, but has lead to high percentage explosive plays down-field.

Blocking Scheme

I have always loved this play as a way to get our quarterback a clean look on the zone read while also adding another blocker at the point of attack. We determine which gap the tackle pulls into by observing which gap is open.

Center calls are as follows:
A gap open = Alpha (Tackle leads up the A gap)
B gap open = Beta (Tackle leads up the B gap)
Both A and B gaps are closed = Crash (Tackle kicks out the last man on the LOS) and Front-Door down blocks.

PST
– Blocks the DE / C gap defender

PSG
– vs 3 tech = block the DT
– vs 1 tech = block to the back-side MLB

Center
– Double team 1 tech to backside MLB - if both DTs are both in a 1 tech in, block backside

BSG
– vs 3 tech = block the DT
– vs 1 tech = double team backside MLB

BST
– Pull to the play-side MLB
– Listen to the Centre's call

The Running Back's alignment depends on his speed. We learned this from what Chip Kelly did at Oregon: if he is faster, then he straddles the tackle's outside leg. This can be adjusted to a closer relation to the QB if the back is slower. His toes are aligned on the heels of the QB and he is full speed on the snap of the ball to the mesh point. The quarterback reads the defensive end's outside hip. If he chases the running back, the ball is pulled for the zone read and he reads the second level for the passing concept.

Over the last five years defenses have adjusted well to the zone read. They have employed the squeeze/scrape technique to squeeze and chase the RB, while scraping over-top with a linebacker to track the QB run. The main advantage of this play is to give the QB a clean look by reading a C-Gap defender, but now this becomes a disadvantage as the defense can key off the pulling tackle. Incorporating RPOs, both on the front door and back door side, allows the offense to use the defense's read key against them to create explosive plays.

Diagram 7-1 Base Dart

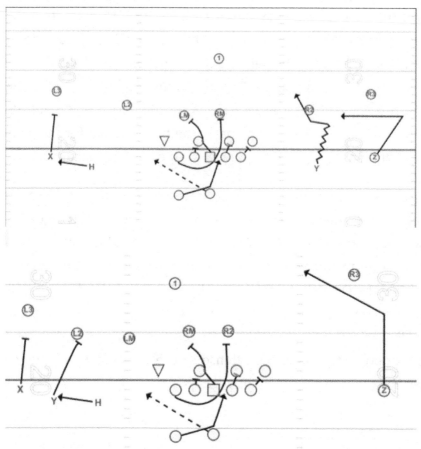

Our base play automatically carries separate concepts on the front door and back door sides. This now becomes a game of numbers and leverage. The quarterback first looks at the front door concept for the pre-snap read. In 2x2, receivers utilize the Surface To Air grass concept slants. If the QB feels as though he can make an easy completion, he takes it. There is no mesh with the RB and he catches and shoots to the open receiver. When we are in 3x1, the single side receiver runs a six-step skinny post to open grass. If the defense reads the pulling tackle, the linebackers will step up to fill their run responsibility, giving the offense open grass on the front door. This can also be tagged with a corner, go, or slant to take advantage of the cornerback's leverage.

The back door is where we have most of our success on this play. The pulling tackle heavily influences back door's defenders, which creates large amounts of open grass. Our base play includes a simple bubble screen. If the DE crashes, then the QB pulls and rolls with eyes on the second level defenders. If the defender keys on the bubble, then he runs, but if he attacks the QB, then throws the bubble on the run. This becomes triple-option football.

Based on open grass, the play caller will tag either quick or intermediate Air Raid concepts to the back door of the run. Below are two quick game examples of how to take advantage of the squeeze/scrape technique and the defense playing inside leverage of the backside with intent to stop the QB read.

Diagram 7-2 2X2 - DART (grass and spot)

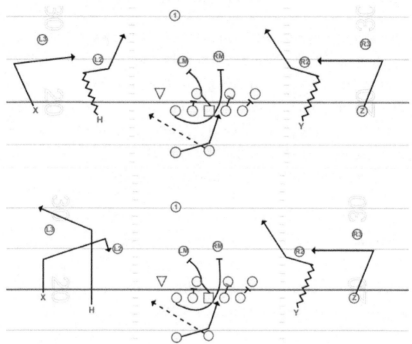

Diagram 7-3 3x1 - DART (stick and hitches)

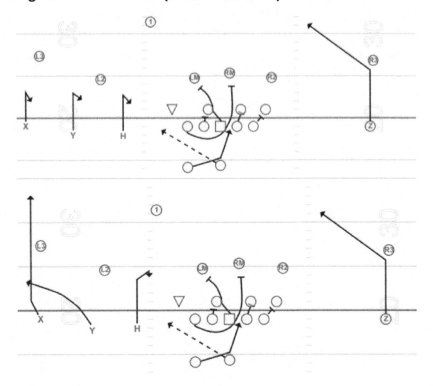

Attaching Intermediate RPOs

One of the most beneficial strategies included in the Surface To Air System is the flexibility of the Sniffer position and what it contributes to the offense. We will either lock the sniffer on the DE or arc block to the second level to provide extra protection for a QB rollout on a downfield RPO. Normally, we lock when a concept attacks the inside of the field and arc when we are attacking outside the hash and want the QB on the run. Again, the pulling tackle greatly influences the second and third level defenders creating large amounts of space for our receivers. Using a Sniffer allows us to further protect our QB on passes while also preventing the DE or MLB from stopping the run. It has also opened up the middle of the field significantly for downfield throws.

Pre-snap, the Quarterback reads open grass, if his read is muddied, he can simply employ the mesh and key off of the read defender. The benefit of this is if we lock the defender with the sniffer, the defensive end is not chasing the running back and we also get an extra blocker at the point of attack with the pulling tackle.

Diagram 7-4 vs Single High Safety (Lock) - DART 9

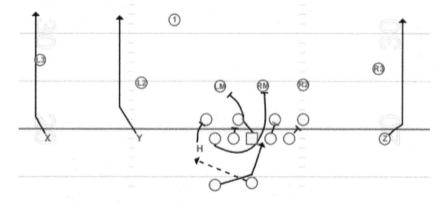

The above image has been by far our most explosive play and against a single high safety is incredibly effective. The QB has a pre-snap read of the front door number one defender. If he is playing tight and the receiver has a favorable match-up, then he should take the shot. The quarterback is told that when throwing the pre-snap, it should either be a big play or incomplete. For his post-snap, he reads the number two defender. If he is playing apex between the sniffer and slot receiver, we know he will be influenced by the tackle's pull and the ball can be fit into the second level.

Against two-high, we should be handing the ball off because we will have an advantage in the box.

Diagram 7-5 vs Single High Safety (Lock) DART Y-Cross

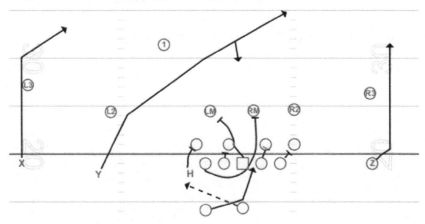

Diagram 7-6 vs 2 High Safety DART Y-Cross (Lock)

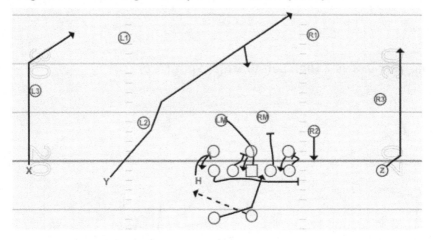

Y-Cross is traditionally our quarterback's favorite concept. The pulling tackle will influence the box defenders to defend the run, opening up significantly more grass between the second and third level defenders. The slot will sit in the first gap past the Center in zone coverage and carry man coverage twenty-two yards diagonally across the field to the opposite hash. It is pivotal that he goes under the number two defender and over the number three. If the safety comes up to defend the cross, the post becomes open for a massive big-play opportunity.

Diagram 7-7 vs 2 High Safety DART Smash (Arc)

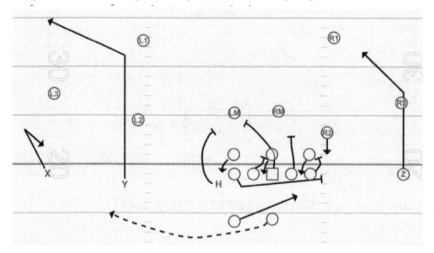

Diagram 7-8 vs 2 High Safety DART Spot (Arc)

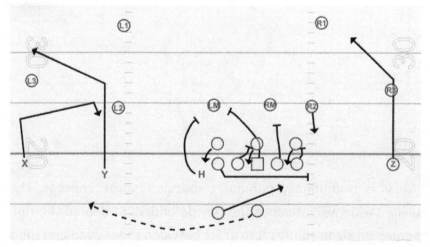

We will also use the sniffer to help our QB roll out and attack outside the hashes. The sniffer will either slam the DE or arc to the number three defender, depending how the defensive end is playing. The quarterback will read the specific defender through the mesh, and pull if the running back is chased.

Variations of the DART

QB Counter

If the defense is cueing on the running back, then the quarterback will find space in the QB Dart version of this play. The QB fakes to the RB, who then blocks the back door defensive end and follows the tackle's lead block. This also locks the defensive front and allows a downfield throw to be made to the front door without having an unblocked defensive end.

Diagram 7-9 QB DART

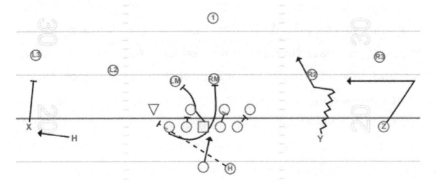

Flipped RB DART

A way to prevent the defense from keying on the running back's alignment is flipping the running back to the front door. The RB will need to delay his take off and not move until the ball is in the quarterback's hands. He then side-shuffles to the mesh point and follows the pulling tackle. The downside of this play is the RPO game becomes compromised with the QB's back to the unblocked DE. However, on the front door, a Now 1 screen can be utilized quickly to take advantage of defensive leverage and numbers.

Figure 7-10 Flipped RB DART

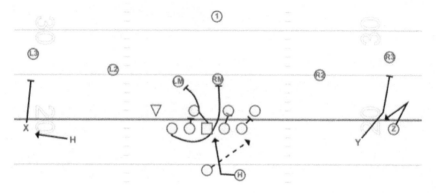

<u>Conclusion</u>

In 2017, we found ourselves getting away from what made our run game successful. With the help of the Surface to Air community, we have found solutions which create more explosive plays and leads to more scoring opportunities. Surface to Air provides quick and easy solutions to attack the entire field, both horizontally and vertically. The methodology for pre- and post-snap reads creates a concrete foundation to simplify the education and fluency of our quarterbacks which has lead to high percentage plays and getting playmakers the ball in open space. The Dart play is just one example of how S2A has helped us attack the entire field.

8.

Jacob Morris - Head Coach Grant County HS - Dry Ridge, KY

Laying the foundation to run S2A based RPOs

"You are the most important coaches in our program!" I say those words every time I see any of our coaches from our Foundation Level teams. We do not refer to our youth and middle school teams as lower level teams. They are the foundation on which the future of our program is built and, as such, are referred to as Foundation Teams. We are lucky to have many great individuals give of themselves to mentor and coach these teams. It is just as important that we, as varsity programs, mentor and coach our Foundation coaches.

Foundation teams face a number of obstacles. The players are not just smaller versions of high school players. A number of varsity coaches have never coached below the varsity level, which can make adapting their varsity RPO offense challenging. A coach may set the bar too high or too low for what his Foundation program may be able to digest and execute. I coached middle school football for over ten years before becoming a varsity head coach, and the following is a guide that will hopefully help a varsity coach lay the foundation for his future players and a Foundation coach looking to run an RPO based offense.

Key one to a good foundation is to carry only as much offense as you need. S2A is an RPO based system. It combines elements of the Wing-T, Air Raid and Option based offenses. Each of these systems have stood the test of time. They are based on a systematic if/then approach to attacking defenses. They force defenses to defend the entire field and play disciplined football. They have built in answers to defensive structures and reactions. One feature unique to S2A is the module approach to building a play call. This allows you, as a coach, to teach a small amount of concepts that can be combined in multiple ways and to maximize practice time which is always at a premium. It helps ensure you are not carrying more offense than is needed. Leaner is better.

Key two of a good foundation is to select what you will carry offensively that will maximize your team's talents. One of the selling points to the wing-t is its ability to adapt to the strengths of the members of a team. It allows a team to feature one to four running threats. Teams may be based on deception, speed or power. The benefit is being able to employ a multitude of quarterback skills and abilities. Using double teams and angles allows the offensive line to handle superior physical talent. You can replace wing-t with S2A in the above statements and everything would still hold true. Some coaches believe that if you are in a spread offense you must have a QB with a cannon arm and speedster WRs. This is not true. If you have a mobile QB then there are many ways to feature his talents. You have a less than mobile QB that can sling it? Then there are ways to feature his strengths. There are ways to mitigate any of your team's weaker features while maximizing their strengths within S2A. Do not be discouraged by your perceived limitations of your players; be infectiously excited about what they can do.

Key three of a good foundation is to coach your tail off. Players do not come to any of us ready-made, though good Foundation level coaching certainly helps. We as coaches must develop players. This takes a lot of patience and work on our part as coaches. I teach middle school students. The changes from 6th grade to 8th grade is nothing short of amazing. We never know how or when a player will develop. Do not allow yourself to place players in positions due to passing the eye test. Place players based on production. Do not force the team into your image, instead help them find their own image. Coach up all the details. Be deliberate with what and how you practice. We all ask the best of our players and they deserve the best from us.

No matter what the opposing defensive coordinator says, defenses on the Foundation level are eight man front base at their core. Defenses will only have a handful, and in many cases just one, way to align to formations. There is no need to carry more than 2-4 formations. Determining factors when selecting your base formations should include personnel (though I caution it being a limiting factor) and run game. I would suggest selecting one family of formations (quads, sniffer, or split back) to base out of and second one to minor in.

Contrary to popular belief, you do not need four true WRs to align in four wide sets. An example would be placing a player who might play fullback in an I-formation offense as an outside WR and placing your typical WR as a slot. In many cases, this would place a larger and more physical player in against a smaller DB. DB's spend time covering and not as much practice time taking on lead blocks of FBs. This would place one's better WR either with a clean release or matched up with a LB that spends a majority of his time practicing against the run with very little time spent on coverage.

Sniffer sets can give the benefits of a TE or a FB in the offense. A coach transitioning from an under center offense will find much of his previous experience can be applied in the run game. He will have access to Gap, Zone and Iso schemes. He will also have access to easy throws to a TE, such as pop or flat routes, which now can be run as RPOs. It is an excellent way to feature a good receiver. In addition, empty sets with a sniffer provide emergency QB options as a way to feature a mobile QB.

Split back formations open up a number of 2 and 3 back runs, max pass protection, and the ability to quickly form into 3x1 and 2x2 formations. This quick motion is also a great tool to be used with inexperienced QBs to give them very clear reads in the RPO and passing game.

The run game is the keystone of the S2A offense. All other aspects of the offense are selected and built to protect the run game. Formations may reduce the number of fronts an offense will encounter into Even, Odd or Bear fronts. Screens, quick game and read options are used in place of complementary runs to punish a defense. These facts allow a team to carry a much smaller amount of blocking schemes. Different backfield actions, formations, and read options stretch the function of each blocking scheme. While the blocking schemes selected are largely a matter of personnel preference, we do believe there are certain criteria that should be taken into account when selecting a scheme.

Every team has a run play they hang their hat on. Most years, that play has been a physical downhill play. The first run selected should be this run. It is the one you believe is the greatest run play in the history of football. If you could use only one run play this play would be it. We have found many times this has been a type of blocking scheme that allows us to either get double teams and/or great angles at the point of attack. Inside zone and gap scheme runs provide both of these advantages to an offense. Inside zone provides multiple entry points into the defensive front and relates to pass protection. It can be difficult to teach for a coach and loaded fronts can take away the double teams. Gap scheme runs are often easier for players to grasp. The extra play side gaps created make it more difficult to be gap sound. A wide range of different players can be used to kick out or to wrap through the point of attack. They maintain their angles and/or double teams against all fronts and can divide a pressure defense. They are slightly more formation dependent. Select one based on your players, formations, opponents and your ability to coach it.

Some form of outside run should be selected. The scheme may be as simple as reach and run, or may have more moving parts similar to buck sweep. A team may recycle their gap scheme to attack the perimeter with plays like power read or using the bash backfield action in combination with another interior run scheme. Due to the complexities of the read game, often, a simple reach or outside zone scheme is more than effective. These schemes are simple, create fast flow which can be taken advantage of and offer an answer to bear or pressure fronts.

Most games and even seasons, a team can be very successful with just two blocking schemes. A third scheme that adds a different tempo to the run attack is a fold, or isolation, scheme. These run schemes tend to hit the defensive front at a faster tempo. A back can insert into an opening on the defense to block a LB just like in the I formation. Another approach is to pull a tackle or guard to be a lead blocker. This category of runs tends to be a little formation and defense front dependent. The drawbacks are worth the gains of a fast downhill run that can function also as a draw and play-action pass, with the ability to read second and third level defenders.

Generating easy throws, attacking defensive pressure, and protecting the QB go a long way in building a QB's confidence. Screens are an excellent way to achieve all of these goals. They are QB friendly due to the target often being square to the QB, and either stationary or moving directly on a line with the QB. They work even when they don't because they force defenders to run. Only average arm strength is needed to make the necessary throws. Defenses will become reluctant to bring pressure and defensive linemen will often play less aggressive. These factors not only benefit the passing game, but the run game also. All of these benefits lead to our Foundation offense always carrying Now screens and either Tunnel or Jailbreak screens in the offense.

Attacking the flanks of a defense quickly and getting speed in space is an S2A bedrock concept. Now screens, or fast screens as some call them, force a defense to match numbers on the flank and place favorable numbers in the box. One should not be deterred from throwing a Now just because the defense has matched numbers. If the WR is given enough cushion a Now screen can still be an effective call against even numbers due the DB not being able to close space fast enough. Now screens are considered outside runs in S2A and take the place of toss sweep. A more hard-nosed   coach may look at a Now screen as simply Iso out by the numbers, or the old Oklahoma drill on the flank.

As Now screens are used to protect the run game the screen and go is added to protect the Now screens. Teams will begin to play tighter coverage or trigger quickly at the sight of the Now screen. It is a simple install that is added early in the installation process. The tagged WR runs the Now screen while the other WRs stalk and go. It is a simple quick turn to the tagged WR, and then reset and throw. There are two approaches to what to do with the tagged WR after the fake. One is to have the tagged WR stay in a position to catch the Now, and to be an outlet if the opponent does not take the fake. The other approach is, if a defender triggers toward the tagged WR, the WR then attacks the grass that has just been vacated to become an outlet for the QB. In all screens, a coach must make sure he instructs the QB what to do if the screen, or fake, gets sniffed out in order to protect the ball and the QB.

Now 1

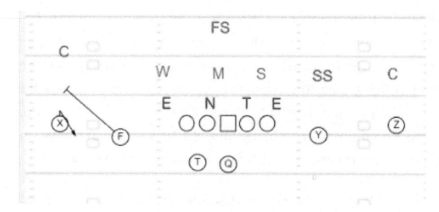

Now 2

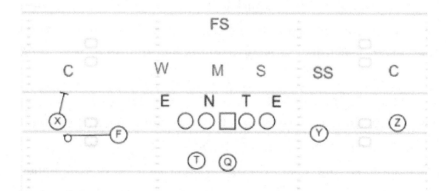

Outside zone Now 3

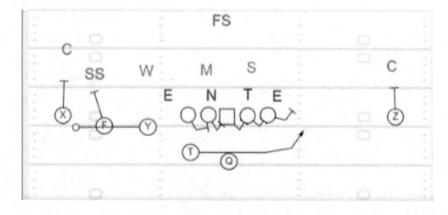

Now 1 Screen and Go

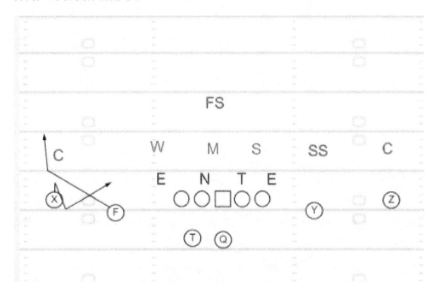

Sniffer empty Power Now 3 and Slant

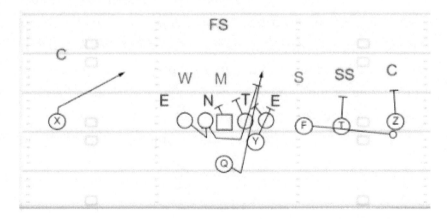

Sniffer trips Counter GT Now 2 Pop and Slant

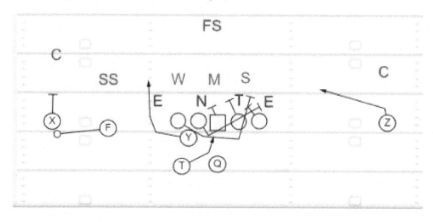

The choice between Tunnel and Jailbreak screens as the second screen carried in the offense is done on a year to year basis. Tunnel is the more versatile of the two, because it can be married to a wide range of backfield actions. It also gives the offense answers when a defense attempts to play tight man coverage to take away the screen. Its versatility comes with the price of being more coaching intensive. Jailbreak is a very simple alternative which works off of drop back action. It is easier to teach but marries up with less offensive actions. Though on the Foundation level it just might be one of the greatest play calls before halftime or at the end of the game. End of half defenses tend to be more prevent in nature, and a completed jailbreak screen, in essence, turns into a kickoff return with the numbers in favor of the offense.

Tunnel Screen 1

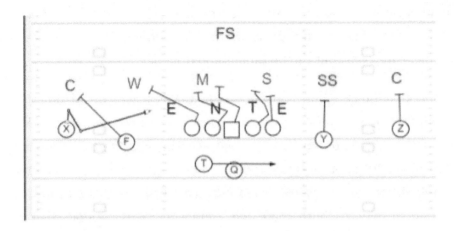

Jailbreak Screen 1

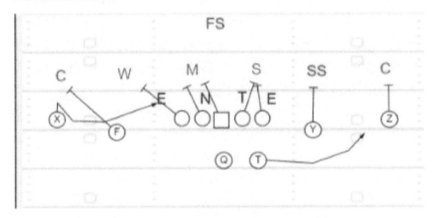

No coach has ever said they wish they had thrown less quick game. Much like the screen game, the quick game is used to protect the run game. In an RPO offense it pulls triple duty as a way to punish defenses that leave themselves vulnerable due to alignment, as a pitch phase of the run game, or simply by being a called pass. There are almost as many quick game combinations as there are ways to coach them. One simply needs to select a few that stretch and attack the defense in the manner needed. Arm strength of the QB can be a small factor, but adjustment of splits, routes, and formations can mitigate much of it. The most important factors are decision making, timing, and accuracy. These are skills that can be taught and drilled.

The first quick game concept we install is a version of double slants. It is the default play side route combination on all inside runs. At times, defenses will cheat according to the tendency to align the RB opposite most run calls in the gun. The double slants help deter defenders from cheating into run space, and provides a solid answer to both man and zone coverages. Double slants keeps with a recurring theme in the quick game of reading the flat defender to determine who should be the intended target. Getting a QB to throw to the front side of a run can be difficult. It is my suggestion that early in the QB's development the coach tells the QB when to throw front side. This can be done through a code word or other signal.

Inside Zone Now 1 and Double Slants

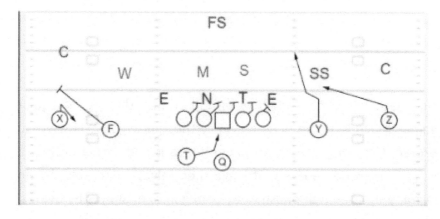

Split back fast motion Counter GT Snag and Double Slants

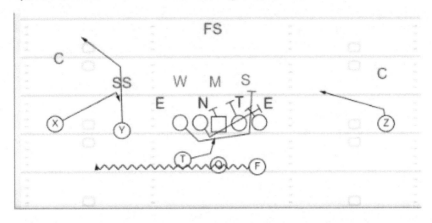

The second quick game concept that is installed is the Stick concept. Bill Walsh and Hal Mumme made the Stick concept famous. It is another simple high percentage throw for the QB off the flat defender. The outside vertical route gives the offense a chance to push the ball up the field. Taking a shot with the fade can be either taught, or a decision placed on the coach. The stationary Stick route provides an easy throw as a pre- or post-snap RPO with the flat route providing an outlet that stretches the defense as a possible pitch phase. Stick is very formation friendly. Pairing the concept with split backs and fast motion can create a very clean read for the QB and pry open holes in a defense.

Stick and Double Slants

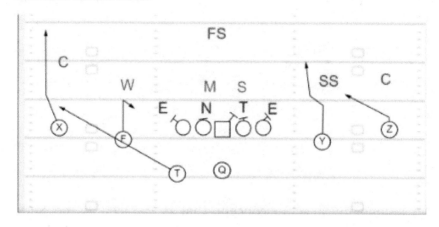

Tackle Wrap Stick and Double Slants

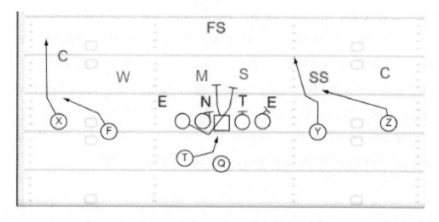

Trips Stick RB Now Screen

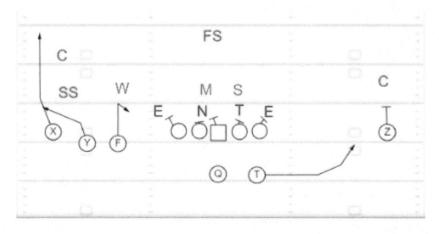

The final quick game concept is the Snag concept. Noel Mazzone has carved up college defenses with this versatile concept. Snag can work as quick game or as a five step drop. The sit and flat combination provides a horizontal stretch that once again reads the flat defender. While these routes end up in the same relative position as the WRs do in Stick (which again makes it easy for the QB), how they get there presents a different set of problems for the defense. It is these factors that make it a great post snap RPO. A high low stretch is created with the flat and corner combination. The corner route also provides added answers to man and two high defenses. These answers allow Snag to also serve as a five step drop passing concept. One important note is that a number of options are available as the flat portion of both Stick and Snag. Bubbles, flat route, and flares are all viable choices to be used to create the stretch on the flat defender. Game planning and personnel should be used to decide which route is used.

Snag and Double Slants

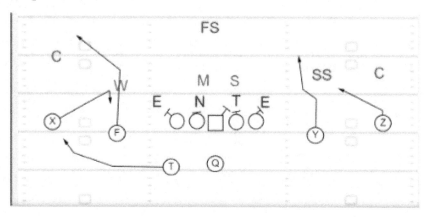

All the components of creating a successful Foundation program are beyond the scope of this chapter. In fact, a whole book could be devoted to the installation, practice methods, troubleshooting, and game planning of a Foundation team. The growing library of S2A resources offers a large amount of material that can be either directly or indirectly applied to these teams. What has been presented here is our approach to introducing core elements of our offense to our future players. It is my hope that this has provided some direction and helps generate ideas that you can apply to your own Foundation.

9.

Sam Baker - Head Coach Grayslake North HS - Grayslake, IL

Leadership: The Grayslake North Way

Leadership and culture are two of the most overused words in the coaching profession in 2019. We define leadership in our program as inspiring those around you to perform at a higher level. In 2013, when I first became a head coach, I knew that I wanted to be more than just X's and O's. I had a set of pillars of success and a mission statement like every other coach that went in for an interview. There were some things that I did really well that I came in with and am still doing 6 years later. However, a lot of it was just stuff my past mentors had used or that I had seen on Twitter, Footballscoop, YouTube, and other coaching books that I have read. I LIKED it, but I didn't truly BELIEVE in it. We had created a great atmosphere in our program that kids loved being around, and we were working towards getting better in the weight room and on the practice field. But then 2015 hit. This year was without a doubt my worst year as a coach in general, let alone being the head coach. We had just come off the first promising season since 2011 when we started 4-1, but we lost the next four. We had a decent amount of talent coming back, as well as coming up. I made the mistake of thinking this next group of seniors was ready to take over and start leading us in the same way our 2014 seniors had. BIG MISTAKE. I made the mistake in ASSUMING they were ready, rather than treating each team as their own. Building a winning culture is driven by the CONSISTENT behaviors that you desire in your program, year in and year out. Then each year each team gets to leave their mark, thus creating a tradition. Part of me wishes I would have known that to avoid what happened in 2015. However, without that failure, I would have never GROWN from that experience to develop what we are doing today.

Love, trust, commitment, obedience

There are four pillars in our program that we will live and die by: love, trust, commitment, and obedience. I got these from our two-time Hall of Fame offensive line coach, who is also my mentor. These four foundational characteristics are not only important for a leader, but for my two children, our team, our coaches, and for anyone. Love is passion. You need to have a passion for your players, your coaches and for getting better. You as the coach need to set the tone and the standard. Tom Herman said in their program they spell love: "T-I-M-E." Developing "love" or passion takes time which takes, trust. If my players, coaches, and administration are not able to trust me, then how in the world can I lead them? If my wife can't trust me, then how can she be married to me? Trust is developed over time, through repetitive actions and relationship building. Trust takes a long time to build and that trust can be broken in an instant. The people you lead need to see that you are committed. Once they see you are committed, only then can they begin to trust you. Following through on your words, actions, and plans when you say you are going to is obedience, also known as discipline. Discipline is not just "punishment," it's holding yourself and those around you to a higher standard.

Misconceptions & False Leadership

One of my favorite things we do in our program is the four step process we follow when electing captains:

1. At the beginning of the summer, candidate must speak in front of the team outlining why they should be a captain

2. Candidate must speak in front of the team at the END of the summer in order for the rest of the team to see their commitment level and their follow through on what each candidate said from the beginning of the summer before they vote

3. Player and coach vote (more so coach approval)

4. Candidate interviews with the coaching staff

We really enjoy this (Candidate interviews) as a staff because we get to see who is comfortable speaking in front of the team. In my opinion being a vocal leader, not a yelling leader, is extremely important. Only one of your captains can be a leader by example, but the other one(s) need to have a voice that the team will listen to in crunch time.

The other aspect of this process is that I can identify the false leadership, or the misconception of leadership, based on their speeches. In the ten years I have been a coach (six as a head coach), in almost 80% of the speeches given by candidates, they will mention they will coach the kids up, and that they can come to them with any questions they have about plays. My thought with this is always...that is why we have coaches! It's not your job! But, as a leader it is my job to identify this and teach them that if a player is too nervous to come to a coach and ask questions about certain plays then the candidate can answer the question. I discuss with the candidates that their job is to demonstrate how to practice with a purpose, to be an example on the sidelines, in the classroom, with their decision making off the field, and what they put on social media. If a teammate of theirs is not doing things the right way and to the standard at which the captains are doing it, then they need to have a conversation with those teammates. The same goes for our staff. However, it should be noted that if you as a leader are not willing to hold yourself to these standards, then there is no way you can hold someone else to the same standard, then that is false leadership.

Boss vs. Leader

A couple years ago one of my mentors sat me down and told me to take out a piece of paper and he was going to read off two items and I was to write down which one I did as a coach. As it turns out, he was reading to me the boss vs leader picture below. I had more answers in the leader column than the boss column. He then told me that I have a lot of great leadership qualities and some coaches on my staff were bosses that relied on authority.

For me this was groundbreaking. He was right. I needed to do a better job of coaching my staff to be better leaders and to develop relationships better. Four years later I still carry this lesson with me. I recently had a coach struggling with relationship building and relying too much on authority. I had a few conversations with him but it did not seem to help (even though this was a difficult group with which he was working). I taught this coach how I wanted him to get better for a few weeks. In the early part of my career I would have just said that coach is not a very good coach and he needs to be better. That would have been me being a boss. I reflected and realized I had not taken the time with him to discuss the idea of being a boss versus being a leader. Then I sent this graphic to my entire staff and had them circle which characteristic on the boss vs. leader side that described them best. This allowed me to review with specific coaches areas which could be strengthened. Now, as we head into the season these are specific things I cannot only model, but also work with these coaches to see if improvement in these specific areas is necessary.

Demands
Relies on Authority
Issues Ultimatums
Uses People
Takes Credit
Places the Blame
Says "Go"
My way is the only way

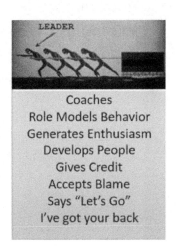

Coaches
Role Models Behavior
Generates Enthusiasm
Develops People
Gives Credit
Accepts Blame
Says "Let's Go"
I've got your back

Being Authentic vs. Too Much Fluff

As the head coach of our household, my wife is one of the most authentic people I know. She is who she is and I appreciate that; there is nothing fake about her. In today's society, with all the different quotes, graphics, and social media, it's easy to get lost in the fluff of leadership and culture. If you truly believe in what you are doing and you spend time promoting it, then good for you: that's who you are. As the leader of the program, when you stand up in front of your staff, faculty, and players you need to be authentic because they will see right through you. You need to follow your core values; for us it is, love, trust, commitment, and obedience. I have always prided myself on being an authentic person. My wife tells me all the time: you are who you are and you don't make any excuses for it (which could be a good thing or a bad thing).

Final Thoughts

Leadership is extremely important and needs to be clearly defined. As the head coach, I set the tone for our program and when we model the correct behaviors and hold staff and players accountable to those standards and behaviors, then we can start to build relationships and ultimately, build a culture.

10.

Rich Hargitt - Head Football Coach
Emmett HS Emmett, ID

Conclusion
(How to learn more about S2A)

The Surface To Air System membership has grown across the United States to include over 40 states in the last two years. We have also expanded to include clients in Europe, Asia, Australia, South America, and, of course, North America. We have seen a proliferation of the system and its many advantages into a wide variety of programs. We have identified and worked with schools that have made the wholesale transition to S2A and included our verbiage and our details to the most minute level. We have also worked with programs that have taken ideas and made partial adaptations to what we consider our full program package. We try and meet coaches where they are, and serve them in a variety of ways, however best they need us. We do not, and never will, force coaches to comfort all that we do and instead believe that the flexibility to put their own twists on S2A is what makes it vibrant and versatile and so successful for a wide variety of coaches.

The camaraderie and interactions that S2A members have with one another is top notch and leads to incredible discussions and debates within our network. This book is another example of the sort of collaboration we enjoy among our membership. We asked our members to write chapters about their own successes inside the system and their own wrinkles that they have devised and executed. This work is exciting for us because our members have put their own successes and their own thoughts on paper and contributed to this manual. We are so proud to have coaches from across the country and Canada contribute to this work and to share what they have enjoyed about S2A.

We are incredibly excited to have our members published in this work, as it showcases what incredible football coaches they are and how they have left a mark on their programs. We have covered a wide range of topics from RPOs, to coaching methodologies, to leadership skills and strategies. It is our hope that this work has enabled you to take something away that benefits your kids and helps you serve your school community more effectively. If you are interested in joining our fraternity and becoming a part of a system that celebrates its members and promotes their success please feel free to reach out to us at info@surfacetoairsystem.com and discuss the system with us today.

Website: surfacetoairsystem.com
Twitter: @S2ASystem and @Coachhargitt
Email: info@surfacetoairsystem.com
Text or call: 615-556-9599

Want more books: Search Rich Hargitt books on Google
CoachTube Courses: Search Rich Hargitt

Made in the USA
Las Vegas, NV
21 July 2021

26825809R00069